Science Dictionary *of*

SPACE

by James Richardson
Illustrated by Joseph Hunt

Troll Associates

acceleration   (ak-sell-ur-AY-shun)
Acceleration is the change in something's velocity as it speeds up, slows down, or changes direction.

airlock
An airlock is a compartment or passageway between the pressurized area of a spacecraft and an unpressurized area or the outside of the craft. An airlock prevents the air in the spacecraft from escaping when outer hatches are open.

Airlock

Inside Spacelab

Aldebaran   (al-DEB-uh-ron)
Aldebaran, Arabic for "the follower," is a bright, reddish star in the constellation Taurus. The diameter of this star is about forty-five times that of our Sun. It is among the fifteen brightest stars in the sky and is about fifty light-years from Earth.

Amalthea   (ah-mal-THEE-uh)
Amalthea is a small, irregular-shaped moon of Jupiter. The dimensions of this tiny reddish satellite are about 95 by 170 miles. It circles the huge planet approximately twice a day.

Andromeda   (an-DROM-eh-duh)
Andromeda is a constellation visible in the northern sky. It was named for a maiden in Greek mythology. In autumn, one can easily see a milky blur which appears within the constellation. This is the Andromeda galaxy, a spiral galaxy 2.2 million light-years from our own. The Andromeda galaxy is sometimes called the Great Spiral nebula or M31.

aperture   (AP-er-cher)

The aperture is the size of the opening in a telescope. The aperture determines how much light will enter through the lens and reach the mirror inside.

apogee   (AP-uh-jee)

Earth satellites (including the Moon) travel in an elliptical, or fairly oval, orbit. The apogee is the point of the satellite's greatest distance from Earth.

Apollo

Named for a god of Greek and Roman mythology, the mission of the U.S. Apollo space program was to land a human on the Moon. On July 20, 1969, the lunar module of the Apollo 11 landed on the Moon, and astronaut Neil Armstrong became the first person to walk on another heavenly body in space. Apollo 17 was the final flight in this program. During the six successful Apollo missions, twelve astronauts visited the Moon.

Arcturus   (ark-TOOR-us)

One of the five brightest stars in the night sky, Arcturus can be seen in the constellation Boötes (bo-OAT-eez). It is a giant, orange star about forty light-years from Earth. The diameter of Arcturus is nearly twenty-five times that of our Sun.

Ariane   (air-ee-ANN)

Ariane is the name of the launch vehicle used by the European Space Agency.

Ariel   (AIR-ee-ul)
Ariel is a moon of the planet Uranus. About 700 miles in diameter, Ariel is crossed by many deep valleys similar to those formed on Earth by glaciers.

Armstrong, Neil   1930–

Neil Armstrong was the commander of the Apollo 11 flight, and the first person to walk on the Moon. On July 20, 1969, as he stepped down from the lunar module to the lunar surface, Commander Armstrong said, "That's one small step for man, one giant leap for mankind."

asteroid belt   (AS-ter-oyd)
The asteroid belt is a huge area in space between Mars and Jupiter where thousands of asteroids are in orbit around the Sun. Some asteroids are not part of the asteroid belt. One group of asteroids, called the Trojan asteroids, share Jupiter's orbit. Another group, the Apollo asteroids, have orbits that cross Earth's orbit.

asteroids   (AS-ter-oydz)

Asteroids are small, planetlike objects. More than 3,000 have been discovered and there are probably thousands more. Ceres is the largest at more than 600 miles across. Most are no larger than a mile or so across. Asteroids may be made of material left over from the birth of the Solar System.

astrolabe   (AS-tro-lab)
The astrolabe was probably the first instrument used to observe the position of the celestial bodies. A form of this instrument has been used by astronomers for more than 2,000 years.

astronaut (AS-tro-not)

Astronaut in Greek means "star traveler."
Astronauts are trained to travel in space,
navigate, or fly, a spacecraft, or carry out
scientific experiments and collect information.
In the Soviet Union, space travelers are called
cosmonauts.

astronomical unit (as-tro-NOM-ih-kul)

Astronomical units, or AUs, are used to measure distances between
objects within the Solar System. An AU is the average distance from
the Sun to the Earth, or 93 million miles.

astronomy (uh-STRON-o-mee)

The oldest science, astronomy is the study of space and all of the
celestial bodies it contains.

aurora (uh-ROAR-uh)

An aurora is a natural, glowing light display in the polar night sky.
The aurora that appears in the Northern Hemisphere is called the
aurora borealis, or "northern dawn." In the Southern Hemisphere, it is
called the *aurora australis,* or "southern dawn." They are known better
as the northern and southern lights. Aurorae are believed to occur when
high-energy particles from the solar wind collide with the Earth's outer
atmosphere. Millions of these collisions cause the outer atmosphere to
glow like the gas in a neon-light tube.

axis (AK-sis)

An axis is an imaginary line through the
center of a body around which the body
rotates. The Earth spins on its axis once
every twenty-four hours.

Axis of
Earth

Direction of
Earth's spin

Barnard's star   (BAR-nardz)

This star, too faint to be seen without a telescope, is one of the nearest stars to our Solar System. It is a cool, reddish star about six light-years from Earth. Scientists suspect that Barnard's star may have a planet or system of planets in orbit around it.

Betelgeuse   (BEE-tul-joos)

Betelgeuse is a red supergiant star about 350 light-years from Earth. It is among the brightest stars in the night sky. Its diameter is between 500 and 800 times that of our Sun. Betelgeuse can be found in the constellation Orion. The word *Betelgeuse* in Arabic means "the house of the twins."

big bang theory

Most astronomers believe that the universe began as a tiny ball of incredibly compressed matter and energy that expanded with a tremendous explosion—the "big bang." This is known as the big bang theory. Those who accept it believe the universe has been expanding ever since the explosion and that pockets of material have condensed to form the stars and other bodies in space. This theory was first proposed by George Lemaitre in 1927. Most current estimates suggest that the big bang took place 15 to 20 billion years ago.

Big Dipper

The Big Dipper is a group of seven bright stars that form the shape of a water dipper. It is very easy to find in the constellation Ursa Major, also known as the "Great Bear." The two stars that form the outside edge of the dipper point toward Polaris, the North Star.

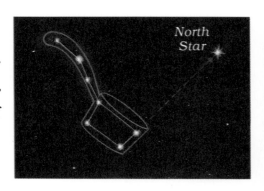

binary stars (BY-nair-ee)

Many stars exist in pairs, both circling around a common center of gravity. These pairs are called binary stars. Very few of these can be seen without a telescope or binoculars, but the star Mizar, and its smaller companion Alcor, are easily located in Ursa Major.

binoculars (buh-NOK-yoo-larz)

The word *binoculars* means "lenses for two eyes." A set of lenses mounted in a frame, they make things appear larger and closer. Most binoculars make things look about seven to ten times larger than normal. Through good binoculars, a person can see thirty stars for each star one can see with the naked eye.

black hole

A black hole is a small, incredibly dense object that is invisible to the human eye. This unusual object is so dense that nothing can escape its gravitational pull, not even light. Scientists locate a suspected black hole by its influence on its neighboring stars. One theory of the origin of these objects is that they are the final stage in the life of a supergiant star.

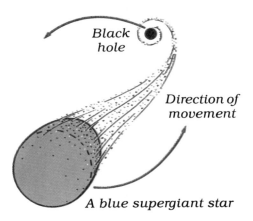

Black hole

Direction of movement

A blue supergiant star

blue giant

A blue giant is a very large, hot, bright star. The surface temperature of a blue giant may be as much as 40,000 degrees Fahrenheit. This type of star may be hundreds of times larger in diameter than our Sun.

booster

The first stage of a rocket launch, used to provide the power for liftoff into space, is the booster. Boosters used by the United States have included the Atlas-Centaur, the Titan, and the huge Saturn V.

Callisto   (kuh-LISS-toe)

Callisto is a moon of Jupiter discovered by the astronomer Galileo. A large satellite, Callisto is almost 3,000 miles in diameter. Because of its heavily cratered surface, Callisto looks very old. It is partly rock and partly frozen water.

Canopus   (kuh-NO-pus)

Canopus is a supergiant star nearly 100 light-years from Earth. It is the second brightest star in the sky. From Hawaii, southern Texas, Florida, and the Southern Hemisphere, Canopus can be seen in the constellation Carina.

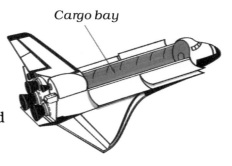

Cargo bay

cargo bay

A cargo bay is the unpressurized area of a spacecraft where cargo, or payload, is stored. Satellites being launched from a commercial spacecraft are often kept in the cargo bay and then released once the proper orbit has been achieved. The cargo bay of the space shuttle is large enough to hold a railroad freight car.

Cassiopeia   (kass-ee-o-PEE-uh)

The constellation Cassiopeia is named after a mythical queen. It is made up of five bright stars that form a "W" in the night sky. Over 400 years ago, a supernova was seen in this constellation.

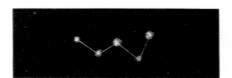

centrifugal force   (sen-TRIF-ih-gul)

Centrifugal force is the outward push felt when something moves in a circular path. You can feel this push when you are in a car that makes a sharp turn. The same push can be used to provide astronauts with artificial gravity in a rotating space station.

Charon   (CARE-on)

Charon is the only known moon of Pluto. It is almost half as large as the planet and revolves around it in a little more than six days. This exactly matches the rotation of Pluto. An observer on the planet would always see Charon in the same place in the sky.

chromosphere   (KRO-muh-sfeer)

The chromosphere is the inner atmosphere of the Sun. It reaches temperatures of more than 50,000 degrees Fahrenheit.

Photosphere   Chromosphere   Solar flares

comet

A comet is a frozen ball of dust and ice in orbit around the Sun. The orbit of a comet is very elliptical, carrying the comet near the Sun, then far out into space, sometimes beyond the orbit of Pluto. When a comet approaches the Sun, the icy ball, or nucleus (NOO-klee-us), begins to evaporate, becoming a huge halo of glowing gas called the coma (KO-muh). Gas and dust particles pushed away from the nucleus by the solar wind are called the tail of the comet.

concave (kon-KAVE)

A concave mirror or lens is curved inward. This is the shape of mirrors in reflector telescopes.

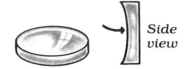

Side view

constellation (kon-stuh-LAY-shun)

Throughout history people have named groups of stars after people, animals, and objects. These star patterns are called constellations and are used to help people locate celestial objects in the night sky. There are eighty-eight different constellations used by modern astronomers.

Copernicus, Nicolaus
(ko-PUR-nih-kus) 1473-1543

Copernicus was a mathematician and astronomer. During his time, people believed that the Earth stayed in the same place at the center of the universe and everything revolved around it. Copernicus came to believe that Earth was not the center of the universe but revolved around the Sun like the other planets. His ideas were very different and not accepted by all. It was nearly 100 years later that his theory was confirmed by another great scientist, Johannes Kepler.

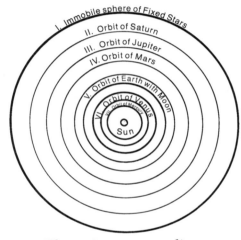

The universe according to Copernicus

core

The center of a planet, moon, or star is its core.

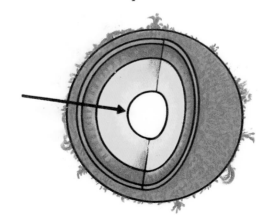

Core

10

corona (kuh-RO-nuh)

The glowing outer atmosphere of the Sun is called the corona. It stretches millions of miles into space. The corona is made up of very hot gas and reaches temperatures of up to 2 million degrees Fahrenheit.

Corona

cosmic rays (KOZ-mik)

Cosmic rays are high-energy particles from space that constantly bombard the Earth. Most are funneled by our magnetic field toward the north and south magnetic poles.

cosmology (koz-MOL-o-jee)

The study of the origin and structure of the universe is called cosmology.

countdown

The countdown is the period of time before the launch of a spacecraft. During this time a final systems check is carried out.

Crab nebula (NEB-yoo-luh)

The Crab nebula is a cloud of gas in space between five and ten light-years across. It is the remains of a supernova explosion that was seen in 1054. Deep within the cloud is a pulsar, a collapsed neutron star that sends out bursts of radio waves. The Crab nebula is about 6,000 light-years from Earth and can be found in the constellation Taurus.

crater (KRAY-tur)

A crater is a bowl-shaped hole in the ground caused by meteorite or asteroid impact, or volcanic eruptions.

Cygnus (SIG-nus)

The constellation Cygnus, which means "swan," is also called the "Northern Cross." At the top of the cross is the white, supergiant star, Deneb (DEH-neb). Deneb is Arabic for "tail" since this star marks the tail of Cygnus.

Deimos (DEE-mus)

Deimos is the smaller of the two moons of Mars. It is irregular in shape and has many craters. Deimos is only about nine miles in diameter and circles the planet once every thirty hours.

density (DEN-sih-tee)

Density is the ratio of mass to volume. If two objects are the same size but one is more dense, the denser object will be heavier.

diameter (dye-AM-ih-ter)

The diameter of a circle or sphere is the distance of a straight line through the center of the object from one side to the other.

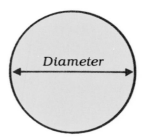

Diameter

Dione (dee-OWN)

Dione is one of the moons of Saturn. Dione is about 700 miles in diameter and revolves once around the planet in a little less than three days.

Doppler effect (DOP-lur)

The sound of a train whistle seems to change as it approaches and then passes an observer. It is higher pitched coming, lower pitched going away. Called the Doppler effect, this is because sound waves are compressed as the source approaches the observer, and stretched out as the source travels away. This effect is also true of light waves. When moving toward an observer, they are compressed and appear more violet. Waves moving away from an observer are stretched out and appear redder. This change is called the red shift. By observing this effect, scientists have been able to determine that other galaxies are moving away from our own, and how fast they are receding.

Earth (URTH)

At an average of 93 million miles from the Sun, Earth is the third planet of the Solar System. It is about 8,000 miles in diameter, and more than seventy percent of its surface is covered by water. Earth is very different from the other planets because it is the only one known to support life.

eclipse (ee-KLIPS)

An eclipse is the covering up or shadowing of one body in space by another body. A solar eclipse occurs when the Moon passes between the Earth and the Sun. Seen from Earth, the Sun is covered up by the Moon. A lunar eclipse occurs when the Moon passes into the shadow of the Earth and sunlight is cut off from it.

ecliptic   (ih-KLIP-tik)
The ecliptic is the path the Sun seems to take among the stars as viewed from Earth.

Einstein, Albert   (INE-stine)   1879–1955

Albert Einstein was a German physicist who, among other contributions, developed the theory of relativity. His special theory of relativity states that the speed of light is the same for everyone, no matter where they are or how they are moving. It also states that mass and energy are interchangeable and that time slows down as you near the speed of light. Einstein's general theory of relativity not only explains how gravity bends space and time, but it also answers questions about the origins of the universe.

electromagnetic energy   (ee-LEK-tro-mag-NEH-tik EN-ur-jee)
Electromagnetic energy is radiation which travels in waves. The waves are produced by disturbances in electrical and magnetic fields. This radiation includes X rays, ultraviolet light, visible light, infrared radiation, and radio waves. All electromagnetic energy travels at the speed of light.

ellipse   (ih-LIPS)
An ellipse is an oval shape, like the outline of an egg. The orbits of the planets, satellites, and other space objects are not circular but elliptical.

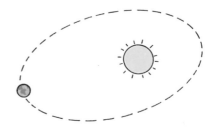

Enceladus   (en-SELL-uh-dus)
Enceladus is a moon of Saturn. It is about 325 miles in diameter and has an icy, fairly smooth surface.

escape velocity   (eh-SKAYP vuh-LAHS-it-ee)

Escape velocity is the speed an object must reach, or have the energy to reach, to break away from the gravity of a planet or other body. To escape Earth's gravity, that speed is about 25,000 miles per hour.

Europa   (you-ROPE-uh)

Europa is a moon of Jupiter. Its icy surface is covered with fine lines and cracks. Some scientists think that an ocean of liquid water may be found beneath the icy crust. Europa is about 2,000 miles in diameter and travels around the planet once every three and a half days.

European Space Agency

This is an organization of eleven European nations that exists for the purpose of rocket development and space research.

event horizon   (ee-VENT hor-EYE-zun)

The boundary of a black hole in space is the event horizon. Nothing, not even light, can escape once it has entered this boundary.

Explorer   (ek-SPLOR-er)

The Explorers were U.S. science satellites. Explorer 1, launched on January 31, 1958, was the first successful American satellite. The purpose of the craft was to measure levels of cosmic rays and radiation in space. It also recorded the number of collisions with micrometeorites, and the temperature aboard the spacecraft during flight. Information from Explorer flights led to the discovery of Earth's Van Allen radiation belts.

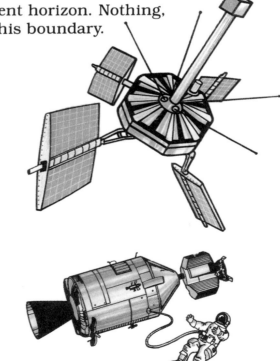

extravehicular activity
(ek-struh-vee-HIK-you-lar ak-TIV-ih-tee)
Called EVA for short, this is any activity of the crew of a spacecraft in space, outside of the protective atmosphere of the craft.

eyepiece   (EYE-pees)

The eyepiece of a telescope or binoculars is the lens closest to the eye of the user. It magnifies the image produced by the objective lens or the mirror.

flame trench

The flame trench is a huge concrete pit under the launch pad. The flame trench directs the exhaust of the rocket away from the spacecraft during launch.

Freedom 7

Freedom 7 was a Mercury spacecraft, launched on May 5, 1961. It was flown by Alan B. Shepard, Jr. Although he did not go into orbit, Shepard became the first American in space. The actual flight time was about fifteen minutes. The craft traveled about 116 miles up at a speed of 5,000 miles per hour.

Friendship 7

On February 20, 1962, John Glenn was launched in the Mercury spacecraft, Friendship 7. He became the first American to orbit the Earth. The craft completed three orbits between 100 and 160 miles above the Earth.

fusion   (FEW-zhun)

Fusion is joining together two or more substances to form a new substance. In nuclear fusion, atoms join together under heat and pressure and generate energy. A star generates energy through the fusion process in its core. In the core, hydrogen atoms are fused into helium atoms.

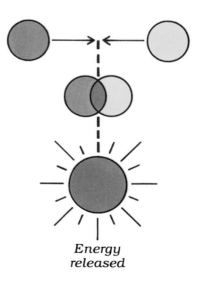

Energy released

g

A g (which stands for gravity) is a unit of force of acceleration. At the Earth's surface, the acceleration due to gravity is one "g." During a launch, an astronaut will feel the pressure of several g's due to the acceleration of the spacecraft.

Gagarin, Yuri   (guh-GAR-un, YOU-ree)   1934–1968

Yuri Gagarin was the very first person to travel into space. This cosmonaut orbited the Earth in the spacecraft Vostok 1, launched on April 12, 1961. He completed one orbit in a flight that lasted for almost two hours.

galaxy   (GAL-ak-see)

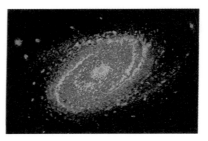

A galaxy is a huge, spinning group of stars bound together by their gravity. Usually, there are billions or even trillions of stars in a galaxy. There are several different shapes of galaxies, including spiral, barred spiral, oval, and irregular.

Galilei, Galileo

(gal-ih-LAY-ee, gal-ih-LAY-o)   1564–1642

Galileo was an Italian astronomer and physicist whose work covered many areas of science. He was the first to effectively use the telescope. He charted mountains on the Moon, observed the phases of Venus, and discovered the four largest moons of Jupiter, which are still called the Galilean satellites.

Ganymede   (GAN-ee-meed)

One of the moons of Jupiter, Ganymede is the largest moon in our Solar System. At over 3,200 miles in diameter, it is even larger than the planets Mercury and Pluto. This satellite has a cratered surface of rock and ice. It is more than one million miles away from Jupiter and takes more than a week to circle the planet once.

Gemini (JEM-in-eye)

Gemini was the name of a series of two-man space flights in 1965 and 1966. It is named for the constellation Gemini, which is commonly called "the Twins." During the flight of Gemini 4, Edward H. White II became the first American to leave his spacecraft and "space walk." The crews of Gemini 6 and Gemini 7 performed the first manned rendezvous in space.

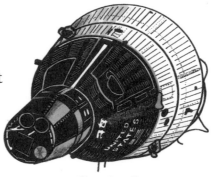

Gemini 7

Glenn, John H., Jr. 1921–

John Glenn was the first American to orbit the Earth. His Mercury spacecraft, Friendship 7, was launched from Cape Canaveral, Florida, on February 20, 1962. Astronaut Glenn completed three orbits of Earth in a little less than five hours.

Goddard, Robert 1882–1945

Robert Goddard was an American scientist. He was the first person to build and launch a liquid-fueled rocket. In 1926, Dr. Goddard successfully launched a small rocket which traveled about fifty feet into the air. In 1935, he tested a model that was able to fly faster than the speed of sound. Because of his pioneering work, Robert Goddard is known as the father of modern rocketry.

gravity (GRAV-ih-tee)

Gravity is the force of attraction between every material object and every other material object, from atoms to galaxies. The force of the Earth's gravity is sensed as weight. The greater the distance between objects, the less the effect of gravity may be felt, but gravity reaches out forever. The Earth remains in orbit around the Sun because of the constant pull of the Sun's gravity on it. If the Sun suddenly disappeared, the Earth would fly out of orbit. See **zero gravity.**

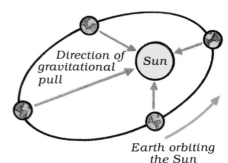

Direction of gravitational pull

Sun

Earth orbiting the Sun

18

greenhouse effect

The greenhouse effect is the trapping of heat in the atmosphere of a planet. The heat is trapped by certain gases, such as carbon dioxide and methane. The small amounts of these gases in Earth's atmosphere trap enough heat to make it comfortable. The huge amounts of carbon dioxide in the atmosphere of Venus trap so much heat that the surface temperature is around 900 degrees Fahrenheit.

Halley, Edmund   (HAL-ee)   1656–1742

Edmund Halley was an English astronomer and mathematician. By studying reports of comets sighted over 300 years and using Newton's laws of motion, he was able to predict exactly when one of those comets would return. He died before finding out that he had been correct, but the comet was named after him.

Halley's comet   (HAL-eez)

The best known of all comets is Halley's comet. It has a small, peanut-shaped nucleus only a few miles across. Halley's comet returns regularly every seventy-six years. It was last seen in 1985–86, and will return to this part of the Solar System in 2061–62.

Hercules   (HERK-you-leez)

Hercules was a great hero of Greek myths. The constellation that represents him is easy to find in the summer sky of the Northern Hemisphere.

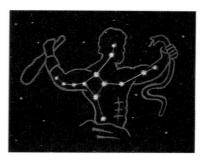

Herschel, William   (HUR-shul)   1738–1822

William Herschel discovered the planet Uranus in 1781. This German astronomer living in England proposed that the Solar System is a part of the Milky Way galaxy and is actually moving through it. He also proved the existence of binary star systems.

Horse Head nebula

The Horse Head nebula is a dark nebula in the constellation of Orion. Its unusual horse head shape stands out against a bright luminous nebula that stretches out behind it.

Hubble, Edwin   (HUH-bul)   1889–1953

Edwin Hubble was an American astronomer who proved that many of the nebulae were actually distant galaxies, and he developed a system for classifying them. He also observed the red-shifting of light from these galaxies. This indicated that they were moving away from us and that the universe is expanding.

Huygens, Christian   (HY-genz, KRIS-chun)   1629–1695

This Dutch scientist made the first clear observation of Saturn's rings and discovered Titan, Saturn's largest moon. He did valuable work in the field of optics and proposed that light travels in waves.

hydrogen   (HY-dro-jen)

The most plentiful and lightest element in the universe is hydrogen. It is the nuclear fuel which powers the stars. Nine out of every ten atoms in the universe are hydrogen.

inertia   (in-UR-shuh)

Inertia is the tendency of an object to remain as it is, whether that be at rest or moving in a straight line.

interstellar   (in-ter-STEL-er)

Interstellar refers to the space between stars in a galaxy.

Io   (EYE-o)

Io is a moon of Jupiter and reddish in color. Io's many active volcanoes spew sulphur-rich material across its surface or out into space. This moon is about 2,250 miles in diameter and revolves around the planet in a little less than two days.

jettison
To jettison an object is to throw it out or cast it away. Segments of a spacecraft that are no longer needed may be jettisoned. In the case of an emergency, the crew of a spacecraft might even jettison their cargo in order to lighten the craft.

Jupiter   (JOO-pih-ter)

Jupiter is the largest planet in our Solar System. Its diameter is about 84,000 miles. If it were hollow, 1,300 Earths could fit inside. The fifth planet, Jupiter is approximately 484 million miles from the Sun and takes almost twelve years to complete one revolution around it. Made up mostly of hydrogen and helium, this giant planet has no solid surface. Its atmosphere is streaked with brightly colored clouds. The Red Spot in its atmosphere is a storm twice the size of Earth that has raged for more than 300 years.

Kepler, Johannes
(KEP-lur, yo-HAN-us)   1571–1630

Johannes Kepler was a German scientist who formulated the laws of planetary motion. He showed that planetary orbits must be elliptical and calculated the orbits of several planets. Kepler also proposed that Earth's tides are influenced by the Moon.

Laika   (LIKE-uh)
Laika was the first living creature, a dog, to orbit the Earth. Laika's journey took place in 1957 aboard the Soviet spacecraft Sputnik 2.

Landsat

Landsat satellites are part of a program to better understand the Earth by photographing it from space. The first craft was launched in 1972. Information from these satellites helps scientists update maps and charts. They are also useful in finding areas where valuable resources may be located and in monitoring crops.

launch

Something that is set in motion or sent off is launched.

launch pad

A launch pad is a flameproof platform from which spacecraft are launched by rocket.

lens   (LENZ)

A lens is a piece of glass or plastic with a curved surface that bends light rays traveling through it. Lenses can make things appear larger or smaller.

lift

The force created by the difference in air pressure below and above the wings of a flying object is called lift. Lift enables a craft to leave the ground and stay in flight.

liftoff

The moment when a rocket leaves the ground at launch is called a liftoff.

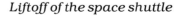

Liftoff of the space shuttle

light

Light is electromagnetic radiation that travels in waves. The wavelength determines its color. Light travels at a speed of 186,000 miles per second. Einstein proposed that it was made up of particles of energy called photons.

light-year

A light-year is a measure of the distance light travels through a vacuum in one year. One light-year is about six trillion (6,000,000,000,000) miles.

Little Dipper

The Little Dipper is a group of stars in the constellation Ursa Minor, also called the "Little Bear." It looks like a water dipper or ladle. The last star in the handle is Polaris. It is also called the North Star because it is almost directly above the Earth's North Pole.

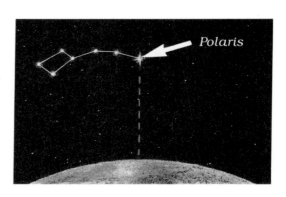

Lowell, Percival   (LOW-el, PUR-sih-vul)   1855–1916

Percival Lowell was an American astronomer who, after studying Neptune's orbit, predicted that a ninth planet must exist. He organized a search for the planet but it was not until fourteen years after Lowell died that the planet Pluto was discovered. Percival Lowell also believed in intelligent life on Mars.

luminous   (LOO-mih-nus)

Luminous is a word used to describe an object that gives off light. The more luminous a star, the brighter it is.

Luna

The Luna series were unmanned Soviet spacecraft designed to reach the Moon. The first spacecraft to hit the Moon was Luna 2. It crashed to the lunar surface on September 14, 1959. In 1966, Luna 9 was the first capsule to soft-land on the Moon. In the same year, Luna 10 was the first spacecraft to go into lunar orbit.

lunar

Anything which has to do with the Moon may be called lunar.

Magellanic Clouds   (MAJ-uh-LAN-ik)

The Large and Small Magellanic Clouds are two dwarf, irregular galaxies. They are the Milky Way's nearest galactic neighbors. The large cloud is about 40,000 light-years across and is about 170,000 light-years from Earth. The smaller cloud is more than 190,000 light-years away and is about 30,000 light-years in diameter.

magnetosphere   (mag-NET-o-sfeer)

The magnetosphere is the region around a body in space which contains its magnetic field and traps electrically charged particles. As the solar wind streams past the Earth, it affects the shape of the magnetosphere.

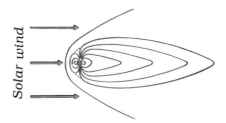

Solar wind

magnification   (mag-nih-fih-KAY-shun)

Through magnification, objects appear larger and closer. The amount of magnification of an instrument is usually written with a number such as 10X. This number would be stated "ten power" and means that things seen through this instrument appear ten times larger and closer than without it.

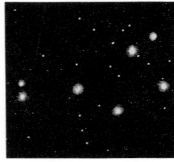

The Pleiades

Magnified

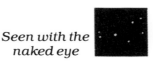

Seen with the naked eye

magnitude, absolute   (MAG-nih-tood)

Absolute magnitude is the measure of how bright a star would appear if it were about thirty-two light-years from Earth. Some very bright stars seem dim because they are so far away. Absolute magnitude is a measure of the real luminosity of a star no matter how far away it is.

magnitude, apparent

Apparent magnitude is the measure of how bright a star looks to an observer on Earth. The brighter a star appears, the lower the magnitude number. For example, Sirius, the brightest star we can see, has a magnitude of −1.5. Dim stars that we can barely see have a magnitude of about 6. A star's apparent magnitude depends on how much light it actually sends out and its distance from Earth.

main sequence   (MAYN SEE-kwenss)

The main sequence period in a star's life is its "prime of life." During this period the star is fairly stable in size and luminosity over several million or billion years. Our Sun is a main sequence star.

manned maneuvering unit   (MAND muh-NOO-ver-ing YOO-nit)

Astronauts wear manned maneuvering units when they must move about in space outside of a spacecraft. The unit includes a rocket kit powered by bursts of nitrogen gas.

Mariner   (MA-rin-er)

Mariner was a series of unmanned, interplanetary space probes. In 1962, Mariner 2 observed and collected data about the planet Venus. Mariner 4 sent back the first close-up pictures of Mars in 1965. Mariner 10 was the first spacecraft to observe and collect data from Mercury. On March 29, 1974, it passed only 436 miles above the surface of the tiny planet.

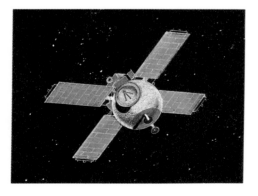

Mars

Mars is the fourth planet from the Sun. Its average distance from the Sun is about 142 million miles. With a diameter of 4,220 miles, Mars is about half the size of Earth. Mars completes one revolution around the Sun in 687 days. In the night sky, this planet looks like a bright, reddish star. At one time, people thought that there was life on Mars, but that now seems unlikely.

matter

Everything in the universe is made of matter. Matter is any substance which has mass and takes up space.

Mercury

The closest planet to the Sun is Mercury. It is only 36 million miles from the Sun and has a diameter of a little more than 3,000 miles. This small, heavily cratered planet has only a trace of atmosphere. Mercury is named for the wing-footed messenger of the gods in Roman mythology because it has a faster orbital speed than any other planet. It takes only three months for Mercury to complete one orbit around the Sun.

meteor   (MEE-tee-or)

A meteor is a streak of light that appears in the sky when a chunk of rock called a meteoroid enters the Earth's atmosphere from space. The friction between the atmosphere and the meteoroid causes heat, making the meteoroid glow. It leaves a glowing trail of gas behind it. This is sometimes called a "shooting star" or "falling star."

meteorite   (MEE-tee-or-ite)

Any portion of a meteoroid that reaches the Earth's surface is called a meteorite.

meteor shower

Most meteoroids orbit the Sun alone. However, many orbit in groups called "swarms." When one of these swarms crosses the path of Earth, many of the meteoroids may strike our atmosphere and become meteors. Their glowing trails can be seen in the night sky as a meteor shower.

Milky Way

The Milky Way is an average-sized galaxy. It is a giant pinwheel of stars 100,000 light-years across. Our Sun is in one of the arms of the pinwheel, about 30,000 light-years from the center. There may be 500 billion or more stars in the Milky Way galaxy.

Mimas   (MY-mas)

Mimas is a moon of Saturn. It is about 246 miles wide and orbits Saturn in less than one day. Mimas has a heavily cratered surface. One crater is more than eighty-five miles across. If the object that had created the crater had been much larger, the tiny moon might have broken apart.

Miranda   (mih-RAN-duh)

Miranda is a moon of Uranus. It has some very unusual and interesting features on its surface. Pictures from Voyager 2 show a huge, wedge-shaped patch of fault cliffs made of ice. These cliffs are about twelve miles high—more than twice as high as Mount Everest. Miranda is fairly small at about 260 miles in diameter.

module

Segments or units that can fit together in a space vehicle or station are called modules. Each module has a certain job. A science module is a space laboratory. The lunar module transported astronauts from the orbiting command module of Apollo 11 to the Moon's surface.

momentum (mo-MEN-tum)
Momentum is the tendency of an object moving in some direction at some speed to keep moving in the same direction and speed unless acted upon by an outside force.

moon
A moon is a natural satellite which is in orbit around a planet. Our Moon orbits an average 235,000 miles from our planet. The Moon travels around the Earth once every 29½ days.

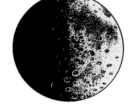

multistage rocket
A multistage rocket has more than one rocket engine. Each engine fires in turn to boost the payload into space.

NASA
NASA is the shortened name of the National Aeronautics and Space Administration. This organization plans and conducts the U.S. space program.

nebula (NEB-yoo-luh)
The Latin word *nebula* means "cloud." Nebulae are clouds of dust and gas in space that may be light-years across. Some nebulae glow, and some reflect the light of the stars within them. Other nebulae are completely dark. Within some nebulae new stars are born.

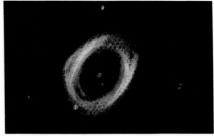

The Ring nebula

Neptune (NEP-toon)
Neptune is the eighth planet, located more than two billion miles from the Sun. A large, gaseous planet, its diameter is about 27,000 miles. It takes 165 years for Neptune to complete one orbit around the Sun.

Nereid (NIER-ee-id)

Nereid is a tiny, irregularly shaped moon of Neptune. It is between 145 and 290 miles across. Nereid is more than three million miles from the planet and takes almost a year to complete one orbit.

neutron star (NOO-tron)

A neutron star is a small, very dense, spinning object that emits X rays. Neutron stars are the remains of very large stars that have collapsed. Neutron star material is so dense that a teaspoonful would weigh one billion tons.

Newton, Sir Isaac
(NOO-tun, SIR EYE-zak)   1642–1727

Sir Issac Newton has been called the greatest genius in the history of science. He worked in the fields of mathematics, astronomy, and physics. He invented the reflecting telescope and described the nature of light. Newton's discovery of the laws of gravity and motion made it possible to understand how the Solar System works.

nova (NO-vuh)

A nova is a star which sometimes undergoes a surface explosion, causing it to shine thousands of times brighter for a while, and then to dim again.

Oberon (O-ber-on)

Oberon is one of the largest moons of Uranus. It is almost 1,000 miles across and covered with many craters. This moon is orbiting more than 360,000 miles from the planet and takes about 13½ days to complete one revolution.

objective lens

Binoculars and telescopes have several lenses. The one closest to the object being observed is the objective lens. It gathers the light, and the bigger it is, the more light that can enter it.

orbit

The path of an object in space that is moving around another object is called its orbit.

Orion   (o-RY-un)

Orion is one of the easiest constellations to see in the Northern Hemisphere. Four stars outline the body of a man and three more stars form a belt. Betelgeuse, a very bright red supergiant star, is near his shoulder. The Orion nebula can be found in the middle star of the sword.

ozone   (O-zone)

Ozone is a form of oxygen found in a thick layer in Earth's upper atmosphere. It absorbs the Sun's dangerous ultraviolet rays, preventing them from reaching the Earth.

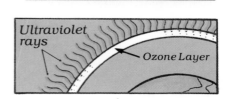

parsec   (PAR-sek)

A parsec is about 3.26 light-years. It is used to measure great distances in space.

payload

The payload is the cargo carried by a space vehicle.

penumbra   (pen-UM-bruh)

The penumbra is the region of partial light within which the source of the light is still visible. When standing in the Moon's penumbra we see a partial eclipse of the Sun. See **umbra** illustration.

perigee   (PAIR-ih-jee)

Earth satellites (including the Moon) travel
in an elliptical, or fairly oval, orbit. The perigee
is the point of the satellite's closest approach
to Earth.

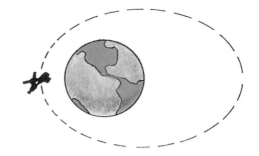

perihelion   (pair-uh-HEEL-yun)

The perihelion is the closest point a body in our Solar System comes
to the Sun in its orbit around the Sun.

phases   (FAY-zez)

Phases describe the proportion of a planet or moon lit up by sunlight
from an observer's point of view. Seen from Earth, the Moon goes
through phases from the dark "new" phase, through waxing crescent,
first quarter, waxing gibbous (JIB-us), full, waning gibbous, third
quarter, and waning crescent. How much of the Moon we see lit depends
on where the Sun, Earth, and Moon are in relation to each other.

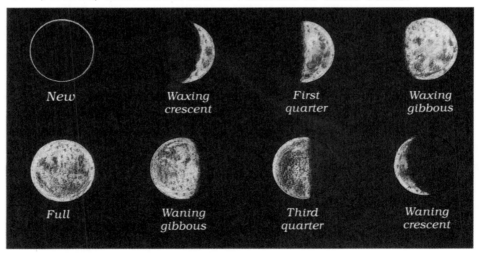

New   *Waxing crescent*   *First quarter*   *Waxing gibbous*

Full   *Waning gibbous*   *Third quarter*   *Waning crescent*

Phobos   (FO-bos)

Phobos is the innermost moon of Mars. It is only fourteen miles in
diameter, about five thousand miles above the surface, and races around
Mars once every seven and a half hours.

31

photometer   (fo-TOM-eh-tur)
A photometer is a device used to measure the brightness or light output of an object such as a star, planet, or asteroid.

photosphere   (FO-toe-sfeer)
The bright, churning "surface" of the Sun is its photosphere. It is not solid but gaseous. The word means "lighted ball." The photosphere of the Sun reaches temperatures of up to 11,000 degrees Fahrenheit. See **chromosphere** illustration.

Pioneer   (pie-o-NEER)
The Pioneer series was a group of unmanned satellites used to explore interplanetary space. Launched March 2, 1972, Pioneer 10 was the first probe to fly through the asteroid belt, and to fly by the planet Jupiter. It was also the first craft to leave our Solar System. Pioneer 11 followed soon after and was the first probe to photograph Saturn.

Pioneer 10 flies by Jupiter's huge Red Spot

planet
A planet is a body in space. A planet is large and massive enough that its gravity will shape it into a ball, but not so massive that fusion reactions can occur, heating it up enough to become a star. Some planets, like Jupiter, are made of mostly gas and liquid. Others, like Earth, are mostly solid rock. There are nine known planets in our Solar System.

To Sun

Pluto Neptune Uranus Saturn Jupiter Mars Earth Venus Mercury

planetary rings

Three planets in our Solar System are known to have rings around them. These rings are made of dust, rocks, and ice that circle the planet. The rings of Saturn are large and easily seen. The rings of Uranus and Jupiter are much fainter and very hard to observe, even with the largest telescopes. It is possible that the planet Neptune may also have a ring system.

Rings of Saturn

Pleiades, The   (PLEE-uh-deez)

The Pleiades is a cluster of several hundred stars seen in the shoulder of the constellation Taurus. Seven can be seen without a telescope and are called the "seven sisters." According to myth these are the seven daughters of Atlas. See **magnification** illustration.

Pluto

Pluto is usually the most distant planet, more than three billion miles from the Sun. This tiny, icy planet is only about 1,900 miles in diameter. It takes about 248 years to complete one orbit around the Sun. Because its orbit is highly elliptical, for twenty years of its journey around the Solar System, Pluto is inside the orbit of Neptune. It is in this position now and will not move beyond Neptune to its position as the ninth planet until 1999.

Polaris   (po-LAIR-iss)

Polaris, also called the North Star, can be found in the handle of the Little Dipper. In the Northern Hemisphere, Polaris always appears to be in the same place in the sky while the other constellations move around it as the Earth turns. For hundreds of years, sailors have used Polaris as a marker in the night sky showing the direction north.

Polaris

Ursa Minor

probe

A probe is an unmanned spacecraft used to collect information about our Solar System.

Ptolemy   (TOL-eh-mee)   2nd century A.D.

Ptolemy, a Greek astronomer of the Roman Empire, was one of the most respected astronomers, geographers, and mathematicians of his time. He predicted the motions of the planets fairly accurately. Ptolemy believed that the Earth was the center of the Solar System. This idea was accepted for hundreds of years, until Copernicus, Galileo, and Kepler showed that the Sun was actually the center of the Solar System.

pulsar

A pulsar is a neutron star with a strong magnetic field that sends out short beams of radio energy in two directions. Because pulsars spin rapidly several hundred times each second, the beams sweep the heavens much like the beam of light from a lighthouse sweeps across the sky. This makes the radio source blink or pulse.

quasar   (KWAY-zar)

Quasar is short for "*quasi*-stell*ar* object." Quasars are not stars, even though they look like them. By studying their light, scientists have discovered that quasars are very, very far away. They are the most distant objects that astronomers have been able to detect and are believed to be the most luminous objects in the universe.

radio telescope

Certain objects in space, such as galaxies and nebulae, send out radio waves. Just as a reflecting telescope collects and focuses light waves from these objects, a radio telescope collects and focuses their radio waves. The telescope translates the radio waves into a visual picture that reveals certain information about the objects, such as their size and distance from Earth.

red dwarf

More than half of all stars are red dwarfs. They are small stars about the size of Jupiter. The surface temperature is lower than that of our Sun and they are very faint.

red giant

An average star like the Sun may shine for many billions of years. When it starts to get old, it will have used up most of the hydrogen fuel at its core. Its outer layers expand and cool. At this stage, a star is called a red giant. After this phase, lasting about 100 million years, the star's energy is gone and it shrinks to become a white dwarf.

reentry   (ree-EN-tree)

The return of a spacecraft into the Earth's atmosphere is called reentry.

reflecting telescope   (ree-FLEK-ting)

In a reflecting telescope, starlight is gathered and focused by a large concave mirror.

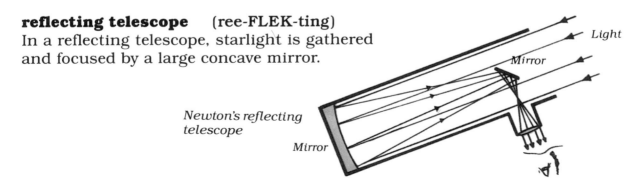

Newton's reflecting telescope

Light

Mirror

Mirror

refracting telescope   (ree-FRAK-ting)

In a refracting telescope, light enters through
a lens (the objective lens) at one end of a long
tube and travels to the eyepiece
at the other end of the tube.
The larger the aperture of the
objective lens, the more powerful
the telescope.

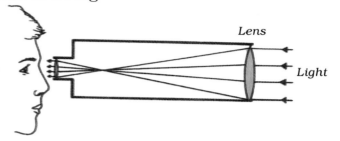

Lens

Light

retrograde   (REH-tro-grade)

Retrograde means backwards. A planet or moon with retrograde motion
appears to move from east to west against the background of stars.

revolution   (rev-o-LOO-shun)

Revolution is the movement of one object in space around another.
Earth takes about 365¼ days to make one revolution around the Sun.
The Moon takes about 29½ days to make one revolution around
the Earth.

Rhea   (REE-uh)

Rhea is one of the moons of Saturn. It is about 950 miles in diameter.
The icy surface of Rhea is very heavily cratered. It takes about four and
a half days for this satellite to revolve once around Saturn.

Ride, Sally   1951–

On June 18, 1983, Sally Ride became the first
American woman to travel into space. An
astrophysicist, Dr. Ride carried out the duties
of a mission specialist on the seventh voyage
of the space shuttle Challenger.

Rigel   (RY-jel)

Rigel, a blue-white supergiant, is one of the brightest stars in the night sky. It is about 900 light-years from Earth. Rigel can be seen in the constellation of Orion. The name of the star is part of an Arabic phrase that means "the left leg of the giant."

rotation   (ro-TAY-shun)

Rotation is the turning or spinning of an object on its axis. The Earth rotates once every twenty-four hours. As we spin in and out of the Sun's light we have day and night.

satellite   (SAT-uh-lite)

A satellite is a body or machine in space that goes around another body in space. The Moon is a satellite of Earth. Rockets that go into space and circle the Earth are also satellites. These are called "artificial satellites" because they are man-made.

Saturn

Because of the large system of rings that surrounds it, many people think Saturn is the most beautiful planet. It is the sixth planet from the Sun at a distance of about 885 million miles. It takes nearly thirty years for Saturn to complete one revolution around the Sun. This is a large, gaseous planet with a diameter of over 71,000 miles, but it is the least dense of any of the planets. If there were an ocean large enough to hold it, Saturn would float.

Sea of Tranquility   (tran-KWIL-ih-tee)
The Sea of Tranquility is a wide, flat plain of frozen lava on the Moon.
It is called a sea because when the astronomers of 350 years ago looked
at the Moon through their poor telescopes, they thought that this
smooth, dark area was covered with water. The Sea of Tranquility is the
place where the Apollo 11 lunar module landed and humans first walked
on the Moon.

Shepard, Alan B., Jr.   (SHEP-ard)   1923–

On May 5, 1961, Alan Shepard was the first
American astronaut to travel into space. His
flight aboard the Mercury spacecraft, Freedom
7, lasted fifteen minutes. Astronaut Shepard
also commanded the Apollo 14 flight to
the Moon.

Sirius   (SEER-ee-us)
Sirius, also called the "Dog Star," is in the constellation Canis Major.
A little less than nine light-years from Earth, Sirius is the brightest star
in the night sky. It is a blue-white, binary star. Its companion is a white
dwarf star called Sirius B, also known as the "Pup."

Skylab
Skylab 1 was a U.S. satellite research station.
It was launched on May 14, 1973. Three
separate crews of three astronauts each
conducted experiments in this space
laboratory. The longest stay lasted almost
three months. Skylab proved that people
could live and work in space. It reentered
the atmosphere and burned up in 1979.
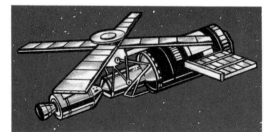

solar energy   (SO-lar EN-ur-jee)
Solar energy is energy radiated from the Sun.

solar flare
A solar flare is a sudden burst or explosion in the chromosphere of the Sun. The electrically charged particles and atoms thrown out can affect radio and television reception.

solar panel
A panel containing material that can convert sunlight to electrical energy is a solar panel. Many satellites use solar panels as a power source in space.

solar prominence   (SO-lar PROM-ih-nenss)
A solar prominence is a huge, luminous cloud of dense gas in the Sun's corona that may rise thousands of miles upward from the surface of the Sun.

Solar prominence

Solar System
The Solar System includes the Sun and all of the planets, moons, asteroids, meteoroids, and comets in orbit around it.

solar wind
The solar wind is a flow of charged particles streaming outward from the Sun in every direction.

space
Space includes everything that is outside of Earth's atmosphere. It is what separates the stars, planets, and galaxies.

space shuttle

A space shuttle is a large, reusable, manned spacecraft. Rockets are used to launch the craft into orbit. The shuttle glides back to Earth, landing like an airplane. The U.S. space shuttle fleet includes the Columbia, Discovery, and Atlantis. Tragically, the space shuttle Challenger exploded after launch on January 28, 1986.

space station

A space station is a man-made satellite that is in a fixed orbit around the Earth. A space station is designed to be used as a base for astronauts who are performing experiments and collecting information over long periods of time.

space suit

A space suit is a many-layered suit worn by an astronaut. Space suits provide temperature control and protection. A portable life-support system is worn as a backpack. It supplies breathable air and proper air pressure within the suit. Modern space suits may be made of material called beta cloth.

space walk

The act of an astronaut leaving the spacecraft and performing any activity in the vacuum of space is a space walk.

spectroscope   (SPEK-tro-skope)

A spectroscope is an instrument that enables scientists to study the colors in starlight. By looking at the colors in a star's light, scientists can determine what it is made of, how it is moving, whether it has any companion stars, and whether it has a strong magnetic field.

Sputnik

Launched on October 4, 1957, Sputnik 1 was the first man-made satellite placed in orbit around the Earth. The tiny satellite collected information about the atmosphere, then burned up on reentry three months later. In 1957, Sputnik 2 carried the first living creature, a dog, into Earth's orbit.

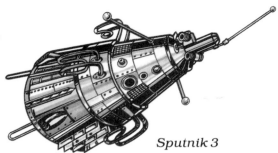

Sputnik 3

stars

Stars are huge, luminous balls of gases that give off large amounts of energy generated by fusion reactions. Stars can be a wide range of sizes, colors, and temperatures. Our Sun is an average type of star.

Sun

The Sun is a medium-sized star that is in the Orion Spiral arm of the Milky Way galaxy. It is about 93 million miles from Earth and supplies this planet with heat and light. Light takes more than eight minutes to travel from the Sun to the Earth.

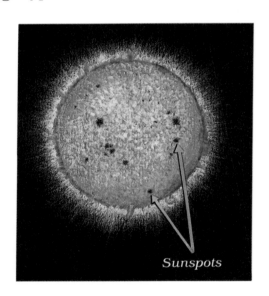

Sunspots

sunspot

A sunspot is a magnetic storm on the surface of the Sun. It is slightly cooler than the surrounding area and so appears darker. Sunspots are usually only visible through a safety-filtered telescope. NEVER try to look directly at the Sun through a telescope without such a special filter. Your eyes could be damaged.

supercluster   (SOO-per-klus-ter)

The largest structures in the universe are superclusters. These are groups of galaxy clusters. Each galaxy cluster contains several hundred galaxies, and each galaxy several tens of billions of stars.

supergiant

With an average absolute magnitude of over −7, supergiants are the largest and brightest stars in the universe. The red supergiant Betelgeuse is so huge that a million average-sized stars, such as our Sun, would fit inside it. When a supergiant uses up its fuel, it will collapse. It may then explode in a tremendous blast called a supernova.

supernova   (SOO-pur-NO-vuh)

A supernova is a huge explosion usually caused by the collapse of the core of a supergiant star under the weight of its own gravity. When the star explodes, it becomes as bright as an entire galaxy for a few weeks or more. A supernova is a rare event in space. One close enough to be seen without a telescope occurs only about once every few centuries.

Surveyor   (sur-VAY-er)

Surveyor was a series of unmanned space probes launched by the United States from 1966 to 1968. The mission of these probes was to collect information about the surface of the Moon and find possible landing sites for future manned flights. All five of the Surveyor flights were successful and sent back TV pictures from the Moon's surface.

An astronaut inspects the Surveyor probe on the Moon

telescope   (TEL-uh-skope)

A telescope is an instrument which contains an arrangement of lenses or mirrors. This instrument can collect more light than the human eye can and forms a magnified image. Telescopes are used to observe and study distant objects in space. The huge Palomar reflecting telescope in California has a 200-inch-wide mirror.

The Palomar reflecting telescope

Telstar

Telstar was a communications satellite. It was launched into space in 1962 to relay telephone calls and radio communications between Europe and the United States. The first transatlantic television signals were relayed by Telstar.

Tereshkova, Valentina
(teh-resh-KO-vuh, val-en-TEEN-uh)   1937—

Valentina Tereshkova was the first woman in space. She flew aboard the Soviet spacecraft Vostok 6, launched June 16, 1963. The craft made forty-eight revolutions around the Earth.

tether   (TETH-er)

The protective line that connects an astronaut to the spacecraft during a space walk is a tether.

Tethys   (TEE-thus)

Tethys is a moon of Saturn. It is about 650 miles wide and has a huge rift valley in its icy surface that runs three-quarters of the way around the satellite. This is called the Ithaca Chasma (ITH-uh-kuh KAZ-muh). Tethys also has a crater that is nearly 250 miles in diameter.

Titan   (TIE-tan)

Titan is a moon of Saturn. It is the only moon in our Solar System that has an atmosphere denser than Earth's. It is a mixture of gases including nitrogen, hydrogen, and poisonous methane. In fact, methane glaciers and methane seas may exist on the surface of this moon. However, the heavy, orange-colored atmosphere surrounding Titan makes it impossible for scientists to get a closer look. Larger than the planet Mercury, Titan is about 3,200 miles in diameter.

43

Titania   (tie-TAY-nee-uh)

Titania is one of the largest moons of Uranus. It is nearly 1,000 miles in diameter and huge canyons cut across its surface. Titania is about 269,000 miles from the planet and takes a little less than nine days to complete one orbit.

touchdown

Touchdown is the moment that a spacecraft comes back into contact with the surface of the Earth after a flight. Splashdown is the word used when the craft lands in water.

trajectory   (truh-JEK-tor-ee)

The trajectory is the projected path of any object that is traveling in space or the atmosphere.

Triton   (TRY-ton)

Triton is the largest known moon of Neptune. It is 2,300 miles across and takes about six days to complete one orbit around the planet. This moon orbits in the opposite direction of most other moons in the Solar System. At a little more than 200,000 miles from the planet, Triton is very close to Neptune and may be in danger of being destroyed by the pull of Neptune's gravity sometime in the next few hundred million years.

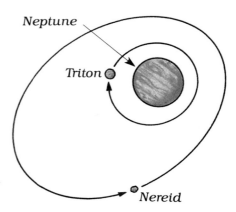

Tsiolkovsky, Konstantin
(chol-KOV-skee, KON-stan-teen)   1857–1935

Konstantin Tsiolkovsky was a Russian scientist. He built the first wind tunnel to test flying machines. He also figured out how to make a liquid-fueled rocket. Although he never built his rocket, this great scientist is often called the "father of rocket flight."

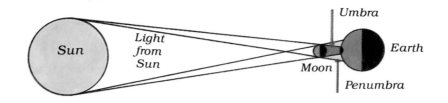

umbra   (UM-bruh)

The cone-shaped, darkest part of a shadow cast by any body is the umbra. Within the umbra, all light from the light source is cut off by the object casting the shadow. When you stand in the Moon's umbra when the Sun, Moon, and Earth are aligned just right, there is a total eclipse of the Sun.

universe   (YOO-nih-verss)

The universe includes every material thing that exists, known or unknown. It is so vast, it is hard to even imagine its size. The Earth, our Sun and Moon, and the stars are only a tiny part of the Milky Way galaxy. The Milky Way is just one of countless galaxies in the universe.

Uranus   (YOOR-uh-nus)

Uranus is the seventh planet from the Sun at a distance of nearly two billion miles. It is a large, blue-green gaseous planet, with a diameter of about 32,200 miles, four times bigger than Earth's. Uranus is circled by thin, delicate rings, but the most unusual thing about the planet is that it is tilted over onto its side, rings and all. Because of this, for the first half of its eighty-four-year orbit, one pole is in sunlight while the other is in darkness, and for the next half, the situation reverses.

Van Allen belts   (van AL-en BELTZ)

The Van Allen belts are two doughnut-shaped regions of charged particles within the Earth's magnetic field which trap deadly radiation from the Sun. They were discovered by Dr. James Van Allen after studying the data returned by Explorer 1 in 1958.

Vega   (VAY-guh)
Vega is a very bright, white star in the constellation Lyra, or "the Harp."
At twenty-six light-years away, it is a fairly close neighbor to our Sun.
The name *Vega* is from an Arabic word which means
"the swooping vulture."

velocity   (vuh-LAHS-ih-tee)
Velocity is a measure of the speed and direction in which an object is
moving. When you change your direction, even if your speed remains the
same, you change velocity. This change is felt as acceleration.

Venera   (VEN-er-uh)
The Venera series of Soviet satellite probes was designed to study the
planets Venus and Mars. In 1973, by touching down on the surface of
Venus, Venera 3 became the first spacecraft to land on another planet.
In 1975, Venera 9 and Venera 10 sent the first photographs of the
surface of Venus to Earth.

Venus   (VEE-nus)
The second planet from the Sun is Venus. It
is almost the same size as the Earth with a
diameter of about 7,500 miles. Many people
thought it might be a likely planet to support
life until space probes landed there. The
temperature is up to 900 degrees Fahrenheit.
Deadly sulphuric acid rain falls in the
atmosphere and the air pressure is 100 times
that of the Earth's. Venus rotates very slowly
on its axis. It takes 243 days for the planet to
rotate once. Venus travels around the Sun
once every 225 days. This means that a day
on Venus is longer than a year on Venus.

Viking

Landers from the two U.S. Viking space probes are now on the planet Mars. After flying for more than ten months, they landed on the red planet in 1976. Both performed experiments, took photographs, and sent a tremendous amount of information back to Earth. The robot landers also tested the soil for signs of life. None was found, but the tests were made over a small area. Communication was lost with the landers six years after they touched down on the Martian surface.

Vostok   (VOSS-tok)

In 1961, Vostok 1 carried the first human, a man, into orbit around the Earth. In Russian, *vostok* means "swallow" (a type of small bird). In 1963, the first woman went into space aboard Vostok 6.

Voyager   (VOY-uh-jer)

The U.S. Voyager space probes have explored the outer planets of the Solar System. The Voyagers, launched in 1977, have sent wonderful pictures of Jupiter, Saturn, and Uranus to Earth and remarkable discoveries have been made. Active volcanoes have been observed on the surface of Io, a moon of Jupiter. In 1986 Voyager 2 flew by Uranus and scientists were amazed to find ten new, unknown moons. In 1989 Voyager 2 passed by the planet Neptune.

wavelength

Wavelength is the distance from one wave to the following wave. The color of visible light is determined by its wavelength.

white dwarf

As an average star grows older, it goes through several stages. After its red giant stage its core slowly collapses under the pull of its own gravity. As this happens its outer layers drift off, leaving behind a small, hot, very dense stellar object that has no nuclear fuel left. This object is called a white dwarf. It shines from its stored heat, like a fading ember in a campfire.

zenith   (ZEE-nith)

The zenith is the point in the sky directly overhead for any observer.

zero gravity

Astronauts in orbit experience weightlessness and can actually float freely. This condition is called zero gravity. Weightlessness is felt when the force of gravity is balanced by the speed and power of a moving vehicle. You can experience weightlessness when you descend rapidly in an elevator or when you travel in an airplane.

zodiac   (ZO-dee-ak)

The zodiac is an imaginary belt in the sky through which the Sun, Moon, and planets travel. This band also includes twelve well-known constellations, which in astrology are called the "signs of the zodiac."

Aries

Aquarius

Taurus

Leo   Cancer

Gemini

Libra

Virgo

Pisces

Scorpius

Capricornus

Sagittarius